If you live long enough, you'll make mistakes. But if you learn from them, you'll be a better person. It's how you handle adversity, not how it affects you. The main thing is never quit, never quit, never quit.

William J. Clinton

Nearly all men can stand adversity, but if you want to test a man's character, give him power.

Abraham Lincoln

There is no better than adversity. Every defeat, every heartbreak, every loss, contains its own seed, its own lesson on how to improve your performance the next time.

Malcolm X

All the adversity I've had in my life, all my troubles and obstacles, have strengthened me... You may not realize it when it happens, but a kick in the teeth may be the best thing in the world for you.

Walt Disney

The friend in my adversity I shall always cherish most. I can better trust those who helped to relieve the gloom of my dark hours than those who are so ready to enjoy with me the sunshine of my prosperity.

Ulysses S. Grant

True friendship is a plant of slow growth, and must undergo and withstand the shocks of adversity, before it is entitled to the appellation.

George Washington

One who gains strength by overcoming obstacles possesses the only strength which can overcome adversity.

Albert Schweitzer

Always seek out the seed of triumph in every adversity.

Og Mandino

Everyone is handed adversity in life. No one's journey is easy. It's how they handle it that makes people unique.

Kevin Conroy

Adversity causes some men to break; others to break records.

William Arthur Ward

A friend loveth at all times, and a brother is born for adversity.

King Solomon

In times of great stress or adversity, it's always best to keep busy, to plow your anger and your energy into something positive.

Lee Iacocca

Israel was not created in order to disappear - Israel will endure and flourish. It is the child of hope and the home of the brave. It can neither be broken by adversity nor demoralized by success. It carries the shield of democracy and it honors the sword of freedom.

John F. Kennedy

Every adversity, every failure, every heartache carries with it the seed of an equal or greater benefit.

Napoleon Hill

For a lot of people, Superman is and has always been America's hero. He stands for what we believe is the best within us: limitless strength tempered by compassion, that can bear adversity and emerge stronger on the other side. He stands for what we all feel we would like to be able to stand for, when standing is hardest.

J. Michael Straczynski

When adversity strikes, that's when you have to be the most calm. Take a step back, stay strong, stay grounded and press on.

LL Cool J

The eagle has no fear of adversity. We need to be like the eagle and have a fearless spirit of a conqueror!

Joyce Meyer

Just as we develop our physical muscles through overcoming opposition - such as lifting weights - we develop our character muscles by overcoming challenges and adversity.

Stephen Covey

Someone said adversity builds character, but someone else said adversity reveals character. I'm pleasantly surprised with my resilience. I persevere, and not just blindly. I take the best, get rid of the rest, and move on, realizing that you can make a choice to take the good.

Brooke Shields

The only good thing about times of adversity is that you realize who your real friends and fans are - and the rest go away - which in my mind is an OK thing.

Pete Wentz

The bravest sight in the world is to see a great man struggling against adversity.

Lucius Annaeus Seneca

One of the greatest gifts my father gave me - unintentionally - was witnessing the courage with which he bore adversity. We had a bit of a rollercoaster life with some really challenging financial periods. He was always unshaken, completely tranquil, the same ebullient, laughing, jovial man.

Ben Okri

One thing about championship teams is that they're resilient. No matter what is thrown at them, no matter how deep the hole, they find a way to bounce back and overcome adversity.

Nick Saban

Adversity is like a strong wind. It tears away from us all but the things that cannot be torn, so that we see ourselves as we really are.

Arthur Golden

Friendship is a plant of slow growth and must undergo and withstand the shocks of adversity before it is entitled to the appellation.

George Washington

Turning pro is a mindset. If we are struggling with fear, self-sabotage, procrastination, self-doubt, etc., the problem is, we're thinking like amateurs. Amateurs don't show up. Amateurs crap out. Amateurs let adversity defeat them. The pro thinks differently. He shows up, he does his work, he keeps on truckin', no matter what.

Steven Pressfield

Let me embrace thee, sour adversity, for wise men say it is the wisest course.

William Shakespeare

Life is truly known only to those who suffer, lose, endure adversity and stumble from defeat to defeat.

Anais Nin

Adversity is sometimes hard upon a man; but for one man who can stand prosperity, there are a hundred that will stand adversity.

Elvis Presley

Fire is the test of gold; adversity, of strong men.

Martha Graham

In spite of discouragement and adversity, those who are happiest seem to have a way of learning from difficult times, becoming stronger, wiser and happier as a result.

Joseph B. Wirthlin

Every great man, every successful man, no matter what the field of endeavor, has known the magic that lies in these words: every adversity has the seed of an equivalent or greater benefit.

W. Clement Stone

The moment we believe that success is determined by an ingrained level of ability as opposed to resilience and hard work, we will be brittle in the face of adversity.

Joshua Waitzkin

Brave men rejoice in adversity, just as brave soldiers triumph in war.

Lucius Annaeus Seneca

The long, dull, monotonous years of middle-aged prosperity or middle-aged adversity are excellent campaigning weather for the devil.

C. S. Lewis

Everything that I've ever been able to accomplish in skating and in life has come out of adversity and perseverance.

Scott Hamilton

To me, obstacles in life build character. You have to be able to overcome adversity in order to succeed and appreciate the simple things life has to offer... that's where most of my inspiration for writing and singing comes from.

Elliott Yamin

I was bullied and picked on because I was so different to everyone else, and I definitely didn't believe or even know I was fabulous back then. But those hard times made me everything I am today. It's all water under the bridge now, but being bullied and going through adversity definitely made me stronger.

Kimora Lee Simmons

Sometimes good comes through adversity. I would not be who I am today had it not been for the internment, and I like who I am.

Ruth Asawa

Adversity is the state in which man most easily becomes acquainted with himself, being especially free of admirers then.

John Wooden

Adversity is the diamond dust Heaven polishes its jewels with.

Thomas Carlyle

There is no education like adversity.

Benjamin Disraeli

Adversity is the first path to truth.

Lord Byron

There is in every true woman's heart, a spark of heavenly fire, which lies dormant in the broad daylight of prosperity, but which kindles up and beams and blazes in the dark hour of adversity.

Washington Irving

Sometimes adversity is what you need to face in order to become successful.

Zig Ziglar

There are uses to adversity, and they don't reveal themselves until tested. Whether it's serious illness, financial hardship, or the simple constraint of parents who speak limited English, difficulty can tap unexpected strengths.

Sonia Sotomayor

Sweet are the uses of adversity which, like the toad, ugly and venomous, wears yet a precious jewel in his head.

William Shakespeare

In prosperity, our friends know us; in adversity, we know our friends.

John Churton Collins

As years passed away I have formed the habit of looking back upon that former self as upon another person, the remembrance of whose emotions has been a solace in adversity and added zest to the enjoyment of prosperity.

Simon Newcomb

There will always be hard times. Use adversity to fuel your fire. In high school, I wanted to play quarterback but couldn't until I was a senior. I played wide receiver instead, and this ultimately helped me because I learned more about the game.

Ben Roethlisberger

In every adversity there lies the seed of an equivalent advantage. In every defeat is a lesson showing you how to win the victory next time.

Robert Collier

Fasting is, first and foremost, an exercise for identifying and managing adversity in all its forms. With faith, in full conscience, fasting calls women and men to an extra degree of self-awareness.

Tariq Ramadan

A prosperous state makes a secure Christian, but adversity makes him Consider.

Anne Bradstreet

Show me someone who has done something worthwhile, and I'll show you someone who has overcome adversity.

Lou Holtz

There is in every woman's heart a spark of heavenly fire which lies dormant in the broad daylight of prosperity, but which kindles up and beams and blazes in the dark hour of adversity.

Washington Irving

You'll never find a better sparring partner than adversity.

Golda Meir

As with the butterfly, adversity is necessary to build character in people.

Joseph B. Wirthlin

Adversity makes men, and prosperity makes monsters.

Victor Hugo

I want to be a role model and I want to show kids that you can be strong and overcome adversity.

Paula Creamer

Everyone goes through adversity in life, but what matters is how you learn from it.

Lou Holtz

As a lifelong practitioner of martial arts, I'm trained to remain calm in the face of adversity and danger.

Steven Seagal

A rebirth out of spiritual adversity causes us to become new creatures.

James E. Faust

When the world is in the midst of change, when adversity and opportunity are almost indistinguishable, this is the time for visionary leadership and when leaders need to look beyond the survival needs of those they're serving.

Chip Conley

I learned to take those experiences that were difficult in my life and in the adversity that I had overcome to use it for a positive change.

Dominique Moceanu

Weak minds sink under prosperity as well as adversity; but strong and deep ones have two high tides.

David Hare

By trying we can easily learn to endure adversity. Another man's, I mean.

Mark Twain

Adversity, and perseverance and all these things can shape you. They can give you a value and a self-esteem that is priceless.

Scott Hamilton

Remorse sleeps during prosperity but awakes bitter consciousness during adversity.

Jean-Jacques Rousseau

He knows not his own strength that has not met adversity.

Ben Jonson

Many of the lessons we are to learn in mortality can only be received through the things we experience and sometimes suffer. And God expects and trusts us to face temporary mortal adversity with His help so we can learn what we need to learn and ultimately become what we are to become in eternity.

David A. Bednar

By adversity are wrought the greatest works of admiration, and all the fair examples of renown, out of distress and misery are grown.

Samuel Daniel

Prosperity tries the fortunate, adversity the great.

Rose Kennedy

Prosperity is a great teacher; adversity a greater.

William Hazlitt

Three hundred years ago a prisoner condemned to the Tower of London carved on the wall of his cell this sentiment to keep up his spirits during his long imprisonment: 'It is not adversity that kills, but the impatience with which we bear adversity.

James Keller

Adversity has a way of introducing a man to himself.

Shia LaBeouf

Adversity isn't an obstacle that we need to get around in order to resume living our life. It's part of our life.

Aimee Mullins

I learned to put 100 percent into what you're doing. I learned about setting goals for yourself, knowing where you want to be and taking small steps toward those goals. I learned about adversity and how to get past it.

Kristi Yamaguchi

Fresh activity is the only means of overcoming adversity.

Johann Wolfgang von Goethe

We become wiser by adversity; prosperity destroys our appreciation of the right.

Lucius Annaeus Seneca

The good things of prosperity are to be wished; but the good things that belong to adversity are to be admired.

Lucius Annaeus Seneca

Comfort and prosperity have never enriched the world as much as adversity has.

Billy Graham

In the day of prosperity be joyful, but in the day of adversity consider.

King Solomon

I contend that not only can you laugh at adversity, but it is essential to do so if you are to deal with setbacks without defeat.

Allen Klein

Adversity is the trial of principle. Without it a man hardly knows whether he is honest or not.

Henry Fielding

One of the greatest gifts my father gave me - unintentionally - was witnessing the courage with which he bore adversity.

Ben Okri

Adversity is a great teacher, but this teacher makes us pay dearly for its instruction; and often the profit we derive, is not worth the price we paid.

Elizabeth Hardwick

People that are brilliant and successful, we think they've just always been that way. That's not the case. Most of them have had some tough adversity in their life. It's prepared them. I've never felt like you could develop character without adversity.

Bobby Bowden

The pressure of adversity does not affect the mind of the brave man... It is more powerful than external circumstances.

Lucius Annaeus Seneca

Prosperity is not without many fears and distastes; adversity not without many comforts and hopes.

Francis Bacon

Prosperity is the blessing of the Old Testament; adversity is the blessing of the New.

Francis Bacon

Adversity has ever been considered the state in which a man most easily becomes acquainted with himself.

Samuel Johnson

He knows not his own strength that hath not met adversity.

Cesare Pavese

For gold is tried in the fire and acceptable men in the furnace of adversity.

George Santayana

Something called 'the Oklahoma Standard' became known throughout the world. It means resilience in the face of adversity. It means a strength and compassion that will not be defeated.

Brad Henry

Friendship, of itself a holy tie, is made more sacred by adversity.

Charles Caleb Colton

The firmest of friendships have been formed in mutual adversity, as iron is most strongly united by the fiercest flame.

Charles Caleb Colton

Prosperity makes friends, adversity tries them.

Publilius Syrus

Individually and collectively, Cherokee people possess an extraordinary ability to face down adversity and continue moving forward.

Wilma Mankiller

He that can heroically endure adversity will bear prosperity with equal greatness of soul; for the mind that cannot be dejected by the former is not likely to be transported with the later.

Henry Fielding

Good actions are a guard against the blows of adversity.

Abu Bakr

When you have adversity and you have pain, you never feel more alone than you do at that moment. And you can be surrounded by hundreds of thousands of people.

Sandra Bullock

I have definitely gone through my ups and downs and faced my adversity and my nay-sayers, but managed to do all right. It is a pretty classic tale.

Steve Nash

I'm somebody who finds adversity is almost as good as encouragement. It's almost like, you close the door, and I'll find ten ways to kick it in and go around it or dig under it or something.

Diane Warren

I haven't always acted or reacted in a way that made me proud, but I didn't make that same mistake twice, and I think that's what I love about adversity is that it always reminds me of what's really valuable in life.

Sandra Bullock

Adversity tests us from time to time and it is inevitable that this testing continues during life.

Walter Annenberg

In the adversity of our best friends we often find something that does not displease us.

Brigham Young

I personally have dealt with any adversity in my life with humor. That's why I told America to 'Read my hips!' on 'Dancing With the Stars' or was happy to play along with Jason Alexander and Jerry Seinfeld in the great restaurant scene on 'Seinfeld.'

Marlee Matlin

I consider adversity being good sometimes, you know.

Brett Favre

Under adversity, under oppression, the words begin to fail, the easy words begin to fail. In order to convey things accurately, the human being is almost forced to find the most precise words possible, which is a precondition for literature.

Rita Dove

Yes, I did shatter my leg, and it really changed my life, in a way. It wasn't much fun, but it did open me up, and as we all know intuitively, adversity can develop resources.

Dan Millman

Those who kept their sanity and humanity intact in the face of awful adversity. Heroes named and unnamed, some known only to God.

Silvia Cartwright

I think that everything you do helps you to write if you're a writer. Adversity and success both contribute largely to making you what you are. If you don't experience either one of those, you're being deprived of something.

Shelby Foote

He who does not tire, tires adversity.

Martin Farquhar Tupper

Very often out of adversity that's when the best work comes.

Tom Cochrane

One thing that I don't think my critics realize about me is that I've been trained to look adversity in the face.

Reggie White

Initially, I know that I handled it worse than she did and I think partly because I've always been... every bit of adversity I've faced up until the last year and a half is adversity I brought upon myself - or the opposing teams have given me.

Brett Favre

I'm not a quitter. All my career, I went through a lot of physical adversity, injuries. It's in my nature to be a battler.

Harmon Killebrew

My fiction is almost always inspired by a character's need or desire to rise above him- or herself. No one is perfect and some of us have much adversity in our lives; it is those people who struggle to rise above their nature or background that I find the most interesting and heroic.

Robert Crais

For Black Label Special Opps, adversity is what you thrive on. General Patton is a huge fan favorite in Black Label.

Zakk Wylde

The overcoming of adversity and, ultimately, denying it the rite of passage, has been a constant and perpetual motive throughout my life.

Heather Mills

I'm a dogged person. I respond to adversity with a steely resistance.

Jennifer Egan

I hope I'm worthy in my dying. I hope I can maintain myself - that I wouldn't become pathetic and needy, and the worst part of myself come out in adversity. But I'm not afraid of it. It'd be such a silly thing to do! To ruin the life you have by fearing its ending.

Brendan Gleeson

A lot of people think I had such a rosy career, but I wanted to identify that one of the things that helps you have a long career is learning how to deal with adversity, how to get past it. Once I learned how to get through that, others things didn't seem so hard.

Cal Ripken, Jr.

These are tough times, and the New Yorkers I have met are facing economic adversity with grace and dignity. They worry about their future, care about their neighbors and hope this storm will pass so they can focus on better days ahead.

Harold Ford, Jr.

Americans have always been able to handle austerity and even adversity. Prosperity is what is doing us in.

James Reston

As a writer, I have this compulsion to take characters who appear formidable and bombard them with adversity until they crumble. What's interesting is watching them rise again, and seeing how they've changed and grown, if indeed they have.

Jean Hanff Korelitz

In 'Gravity,' nearly everything is a metaphor for the main character. The way I tend to approach a film is that character and background are equally important; one informs the other. Here, Sandra Bullock is caught between Earth and the void of the universe, just floating there in between. We use the debris as a metaphor for adversity.

Alfonso Cuaron

Adversity is simply part of earth life. From it we can grow and progress if we choose to. Yes, some trials come because of our own disobedience, but many trials are simply part of life.

John Bytheway

If you ask me why I've succeeded, it's because I was in the Royal Marines. You have this unbelievable sense of achievement and of overcoming adversity. That's the confidence it breeds.

Brian McDermott

At key crossroads in his life, Vernon Davis has continued to make a conscious choice to grow as a person and player. His determination through adversity since his childhood days is commendable.

Hannah Storm

The human race has had long experience and a fine tradition in surviving adversity. But we now face a task for which we have little experience, the task of surviving prosperity.

Alan Gregg

In times of adversity - for the country we love - Maryland always chooses to move forward. Progress is a choice. Job creation is a choice. Whether we move forward or back: this too is a choice.

Martin O'Malley

I get Tweets every day from people telling me that 'Hey, I'm going to overcome my injury or my illness. Cancer. Different diseases. I can beat it because Adrian Peterson showed me the determination and the willpower to be able to prosper and get through adversity whenever it comes.'

Adrian Peterson

I look at adversity to not keep me down long. We are human, so we do go through pain and we struggle with things, but it's all about how you respond to a situation. My whole life, I've been responding in a positive way and keeping a positive mind, keeping God first in my heart, in my mind. No matter what wrong I've done, I know who sees the heart.

Adrian Peterson

I studied in Britain and spent great moments of my life there as a student living in Belsize Park. I admire the British trait of the stiff upper lip in the face of adversity. My wife studied in Britain, too, and both of us have many friends there.

Asif Ali Zardari

In so many things, growth comes from adversity.

Michael Huffington

Adversity has the same effect on a man that severe training has on the pugilist: it reduces him to his fighting weight.

Josh Billings

He knows not his own strength who hath not met adversity.

William Samuel Johnson

It feels good when guys reach out to be inspired - and you have shown people an example of how you can come back and be better than you were before when adversity strikes; and when the world predicts the opposite, you show them you not only can be successful but be great.

Adrian Peterson

Adversity leads us to think properly of our state, and so is most beneficial to us.

Samuel Johnson

I'll say this for adversity: people seem to be able to stand it, and that's more than I can say for prosperity.

Kin Hubbard

You may feel singled out when adversity enters your life. You shake your head and wonder, 'Why me?'

Joseph B. Wirthlin

The experience of democracy is like the experience of life itself-always changing, infinite in its variety, sometimes turbulent and all the more valuable for having been tested by adversity.

Jimmy Carter

I didn't care what, how much adversity life threw at me. I intended to get to the top.

Ted Turner

Without adversity a person hardly knows whether they are honest or not.

Henry Fielding

I don't think we live in those times when great art comes out of great adversity.

Noel Gallagher

You know, you have to have some inner philosophy to deal with adversity.

Kirk Douglas

A man is insensible to the relish of prosperity until he has tasted adversity.

Rosalind Russell

Whenever I do the sign of the cross, it always brings comfort in situations when you are faced with adversity and stress.

Troy Polamalu

Adversity is a stimulus.

James Broughton

I wish that only three residents of Tel Aviv could see what conditions on the West Bank are like. Living in such proximity, most Israelis have no idea about the adversity on the West Bank.

Zubin Mehta

Seven and half years ago I began my own journey. For me and my family it was a time of adversity. But during that adversity I derived a deeper faith. And born out of that adversity was a commitment to devote myself to those people and to those issues that truly matter to me.

Paul Tsongas

I work best when there is adversity: I seem to get calmer the more the fur is flying.

Andrea Arnold

Grit your teeth and smile. In the face of adversity, go. They don't deserve you.

Christine Lagarde

I try not to get too low. I fight adversity as hard as I can fight it, not to get too low. When good things happen, I don't really embrace it. I just say it's a lucky day.

Rick Pitino

What really grabs me is when a reader writes to express her personal story and how a book helped her situation, or her acceptance of a situation she can't change. I read some sad cases in my snail and electronic mail. I respond to all I can, affirming that they are the true heroes of life because they are fighting through adversity and surviving.

Lurlene McDaniel

Whenever people are faced with any sort of adversity... they tend to gravitate toward things that make them comfortable, and things that they feel are important.

Grant Achatz

Funnily enough, I did a play called 'Jumpy' on the West End before I did 'Divergent,' and there was an essence of that character I played, called Cam, in Will. In the sense of his vulnerability, and... he had a sense of humor that comes out of adversity, similar to Will.

Ben Lloyd-Hughes

I think really what I'm saying is that I thrive on adversity.

Richard Marx

I am a quiet man who grows through adversity.

Jose Maria Aznar

I desire an special interest in your prayers that my faith fail not in the day of adversity.

John Hawley

I tend to not discriminate when it comes to people I can learn from. Basically, if someone has built a meaningful business in software, technology or media, faced disruption and adversity, and overcame underdog status, I want to know how they did it.

Aaron Levie

You don't play 162 games without facing some adversity during the course of the year.

Tom Glavine

Of course, losing my father was traumatic. I was an only child. But from the time my father died, my general theme in life has been to turn adversity into opportunity.

Thomas G. Stemberg

Whatever changes the new era brings, whatever new pathways we take, I am sure that our special relationship with America - forged in adversity, will not change.

Mary McAleese

Remember the great adversity of art or anything else is a hurried life.

Robert James Waller

Constant success shows us but one side of the world; adversity brings out the reverse of the picture.

Charles Caleb Colton

I'm able to make decisions even in the face of adversity.

Nikki Sixx

The Adversity Index was created by msnbc.com and Moody's Analytics to track the economic fortunes of states and metro areas. Each month, the Adversity Index uses government data on employment, industrial production, housing starts and home prices to label each area as expanding, at risk of recession, in recession or recovering.

Bill Dedman

You don't want people who have never had to deal with adversity - you want people who have been able to deal successfully with adversity. That's what adds to society. Those are going to be the hardest-working, best people.

Linda Ronstadt

I'm used to adversity and working really well in difficult situations. It was hard for me to accept the success.

Paula Cole